RIZZOLI
NEW YORK

Louis Féraud

The following people have worked together on this project:
Michel Baraquand, Malgosia Guedj, Pierre-Yves Guillen, Gilles
Lambert, Emma Staffelbach, Marie-José Treichler, Hubertus von
Gemmingen.

Photographs by: David Bailey, Pier Blattner, Jean-Paul Cadé, Lucien
Clergue, Pierre Derly, Just Jaekin, Hervé Nabon, Christian Riviéré.

Drawings by: Helga Björnsson, Caroline Field, Bernard Mainardi.
Art Director: **Gilles Néret.**

French-language edition: **Louis Féraud**
Copyright ©1985 by Société Louis-Féraud SA, Paris (France) and
Office du Livre SA, Fribourg (Switzerland)

English text by André-François Villon
Copyright ©1986 by Société Louis-Féraud SA, Paris (France) and
Office du Livre SA, Fribourg (Switzerland)

English translation published in 1986 in the United States of America by:

*R*IZZOLI INTERNATIONAL PUBLICATIONS, INC.
597 Fifth Avenue/New York 10017

Library of Congress Catalogue Card Number: 85-62404

ISBN: 0-8478-0683-9

This book was printed in September 1985 by Graphische Betriebe NZZ
Fretz AG, Zurich.
Setting: Allprint AG, Zurich, Photolithographs: Eurocrom 4, Treviso.
Binding: Burkhardt AG, S.A., Mönchaltorf-Zurich.
Production: Emma Staffelbach.
Editorial coordination: Marie-José Treichler, Barbara Perroud-Benson.

Printed and bound in Switzerland

contents

To Zizi
To Lilo

For Women, by Design

As far back as I can remember, I have always been crazy about women. Even before I knew how to say "Mama," I could tell immediately when a woman had entered the room, and I instinctively knew how essential women would be to me. I had barely learned how to walk when I experienced my first heartbreak – my first love, my nanny, went away, and I couldn't stop crying. Six years later I fell in love with Anna. She had come to spend her vacation in the house next door to us in the little town of Arles. Although I have no recollection of what she looked like or how she dressed, I can still remember her soft eyes and sweet laughter. But by the end of the summer, when it came time to harvest the grapes, she also left, and again I felt lonely and abandoned.

My life had hardly begun, and I felt already that women were somehow inaccessible. Little did I suspect that my entire life would be devoted to finding ways to keep them from leaving. What I have accomplished has been out of love for women. Looking back, I don't think I ever consciously considered "couture" as my chosen "métier." How could I? For me it came naturally; it was the one way to make sure that I would be surrounded by women all of the time.

The only recollection I have of the clothes I wore in my early childhood in Arles is of the little black velvet jacket I wore on special occasions. Trimmed in black silk and worn over a white shirt with ruffles and a snug vest, it was and still is the traditional outfit of the "gardians," the cowboys of the Camargue who race their white ponies through the marshes on the Rhône River delta. I learned my first lesson in style from the "gardians."

Years later I opened my first boutique in Cannes, on the sun-drenched Côte d'Azur. That's where it all really started – with Brigitte Bardot. Photographers and journalists chased her everywhere; women copied her; and I tried in vain to seduce her. I finally succeeded, with one of my white piqué dresses, its white lace collar revealing just enough of her beautiful, tanned shoulders. Within a week, from the Croisette in Cannes to the Promenade des Anglais in Nice, from Monte Carlo all the way down to Capri, every woman in sight was wearing my white piqué dress. We sold 500 of them in a matter of days.

It was my first success, and my first panic. Our little workshop could not keep up with the orders. That little white dress had forced us into the big time. My wife Zizi and I were only twenty-five years old. Now we had to face Paris and the textile industry. Paris scared

Opposite, knitted coat in black and white checkerboard weave, trimmed in mink, 1980. Taken in front of the Elysée Palace, opposite the Féraud fashion house on the rue du Faubourg Saint Honoré; also pictured is a member of the French President's elite bodyguard, the Garde Républicaine.

Pages 6–7, embroidered silk evening gown, beaded and feathered with matching chiffon shawl, stitched with precious stones.

Pages 8–9, "We exchanged the blue Mediterranean for a view of the presidential palace, the Elysée."

both of us. It would have been easier to face sailing a boat around the world on the open sea. But instead of a sailboat, what we decided on was a small shop at number 88 rue du Faubourg Saint Honoré, at the hub of the "haute couture" industry in Paris.

We exchanged the blue Mediterranean for a view of the presidential palace, the Elysée, from the window of the tiny workshop above the boutique. Downstairs the shop was bedlam: Customers pushed their way in to buy dresses faster than we could produce them, and it took a while before our original staff of forty from Cannes managed to adjust to the frenetic pace of Paris.

Ingrid Bergman, Liz Taylor, Richard Burton, Kim Novak, and other stars soon began coming to us, and we went to them: We did the wardrobes for at least a dozen films in the early days. After the initial storm of success, it was smooth sailing for us on the Faubourg Saint Honoré until 1960, when we decided we were ready to embark on a more perilous course and present a "couture" collection. Preparing a collection – especially for the first time – is a monumental and insane undertaking. We threw ourselves into it with passion, thinking all we would need was needles, thread, and a showroom. In the process we discovered that patience was helpful as well.

My friends, many of them journalists, still remind me of that first collection. They can even describe it in detail. I always listen to them in disbelief: Somehow, I don't remember it in quite the same way as they do. I seem to recall that there were only a handful of people there, and I was certain at the time that the press had gone to the wrong address. Oleg Cassini, my American colleague and a confidant of Jackie Kennedy, just happened by; he had been strolling down the Faubourg when one of my friends practically dragged him in. He liked the collection so much that he offered us a contract on the spot. I signed without even reading it: we were young and carefree.

At that time "couture" was considered an exclusively Parisian endeavor, so I could hardly have guessed then that I would be crossing oceans more often than I do the Seine; but I soon learned how important our friends and partners abroad would be to the success of our house. From the time of my very first collection, I decided to share the Féraud label with friends in Germany, Italy, Japan, and America, each country contributing its own special talents to our international line.

In 1958 we began granting licenses to foreign manufacturers, starting with the United States and Japan. I entrusted Americans with

Matadors prepare the bull in the opening moments of a bull-fight in the Roman arena at Arles. Photographed by Lucien Clergue.

The Arlésiennes – the best dressed women in the world.

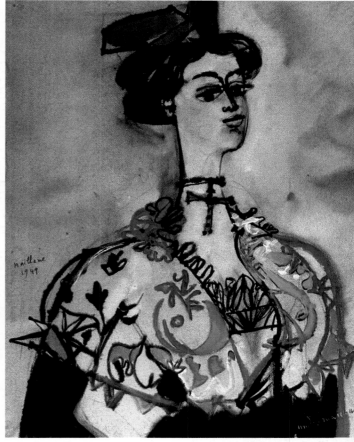

Women of Arles –
"Arlésiennes" – in their
traditional laces. The
"Arlésienne" – also
immortalized in a Bizet opera
like her cousin Carmen –
could drive a man to
distraction.

Above, "Arlésienne" by the
painter Marchand.

Louis Féraud's studio in Paris.

Pages 20–21, "The Old Man and the Tropical Sea," painted by Louis Féraud in 1958; superimposed, a silk dress, printed by Duroux in Lyons, 1979.

my perfume collection, while Seiji Tsutsumi, a poet, became my partner in Japan. When he is not producing the Féraud line he writes witty haiku verses that are widely admired and have been translated into several languages. He also happens to own the Tokyo subway. By 1968 Mexico, Brazil, Argentina, and Australia had joined our team, and our collections were being shown to thousands of people around the world. Eventually we had granted over a hundred licenses to foreign companies. At times we even lost track of how many enterprises were involved, but we never worried. Our foreign partnerships paid off, and we still controlled the creative spark: Our collections were successful. But despite our triumphs at home and abroad, we have still managed to retain the feeling of nonchalance that has characterized the Maison Féraud from the very beginning.

In 1970, faced in Brazil with the dilemma of not being allowed to export the cruzeiros we were earning as fast as inflation was swallowing them up, I decided to invest the money in a farm there. A "fazenda" was for sale in the state of Mato Grosso near the border of Paraguay: 100,000 acres of fertile land, with a standing farmhouse and 30,000 head of cattle. It belonged to an Italian family that owned a "prêt à porter" industry in São Paulo where 300 people turned out a Louis Féraud Brazilian line with a distinctly Italian flavor.

When I first visited the factory, I was received like a prince. We drank Brazilian champagne and danced the samba in the workshops. I decided to visit the farm with my second wife Mia, who is American, and two of our models also came along. The trip nearly ended in disaster. En route to the "fazenda" our boat capsized in a tropical

river – one without piranhas, fortunately! – and we were forced to
drift downstream for ten miles, clinging to the boat's hull. We had
practically given up hope when, at last, a group of Indians overcame
their astonishment at seeing us there, pulled us out of the water, and
offered us their huts for the night. The Indians were dressed with
natural simplicity and elegance, and I noticed what beautiful bone and
leather jewelry the women wore. I think this was the first time I
recognized the importance of accessories, and since then I have
developed a taste for bold bracelets and bangles (although I
abandoned the idea of buying the "fazenda").

Back in the United States, our association with Saks Fifth Avenue
continued to prosper, while in England the situation was,
characteristically, unusual. At first we had two main partners there:
the Peters Brothers (specializing in manufacturing coats and skirts)
and Berney (England's largest dress manufacturer) whom we
nicknamed the "Red Baron." A genuine English eccentric, Berney
would travel only in his single-seater plane, which he piloted himself
in all weathers, of course. Everytime a plane flew overhead or a bee
buzzed in the window, we would remember with a shudder our
daredevil English partner. According to the agreement, our British
partners had the right to use the Féraud label in all of Great Britain's
former dominions, and thanks to them we opened shops in most of
the Commonwealth nations.

Around that time I had the absurd idea of single-handedly
launching my own perfume. For this ill-fated venture it seemed that
all the money in the world would not suffice, and the result was that I

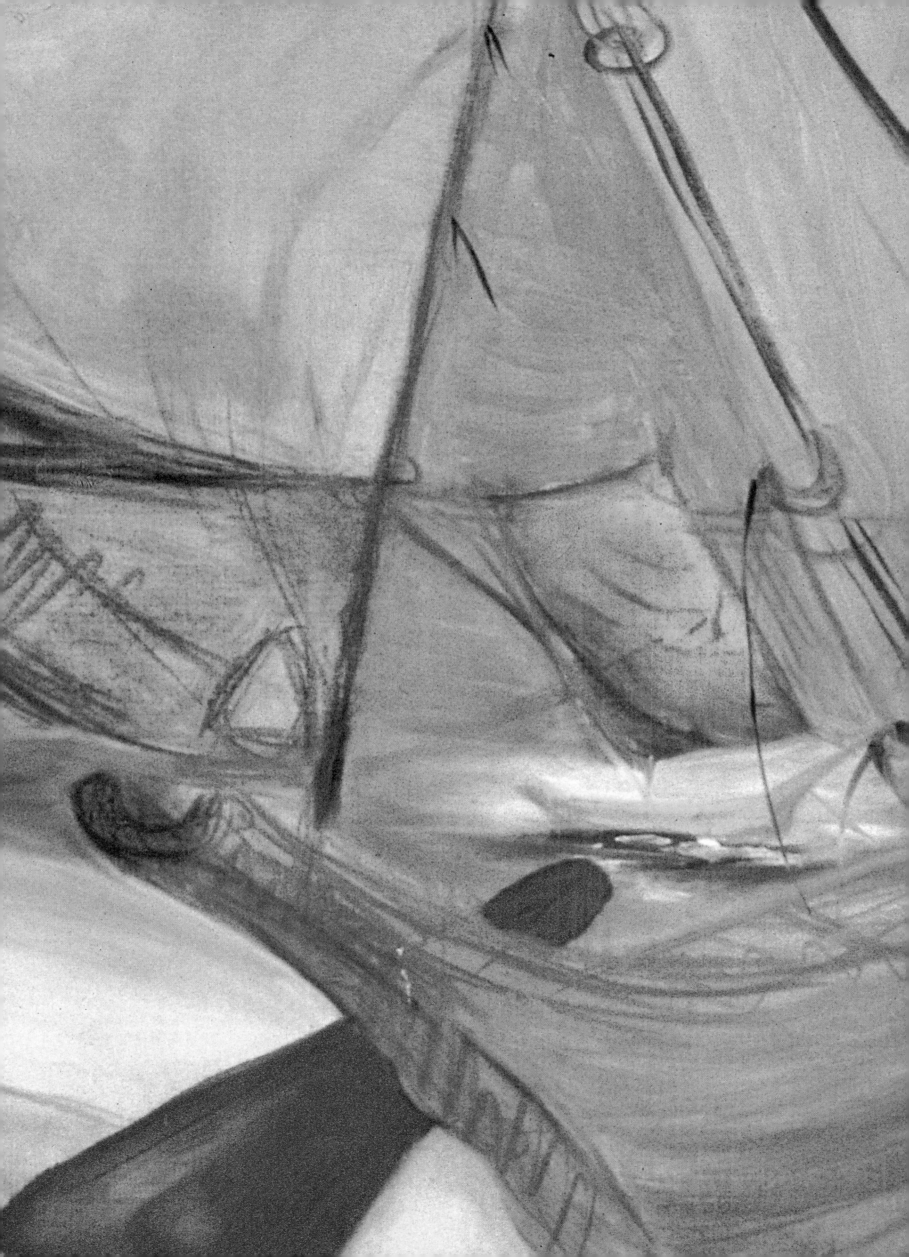

Study for patterns by Helga.
Fall/Winter Collection
1985–86.

Opposite, the peasant dress
was created eight years ago
for a collection inspired by my
French provincial background.
A blend of three different
prints, it was a royal trinket.

Pages 22–23, matching silk
jackets, blouses, skirt-culottes,
photographed by David Bailey
to promote Avon's new
perfume "Fantasque," 1981.
David Bailey, husband, then
lover of Catherine Deneuve
(whose sister Françoise
Dorléac was our star model),
made faces at his models to
help them relax. These
casually elegant ensembles
appear to have no seams –
perfectly suited for the office
or lunch at "Maxims".

Pages 24–25, three dresses
from left to right: a
hand-painted ensemble with
matching jacket (1981), a
blue and white print on crêpe
de Chine by Duroux (1979)
and a printed and
embroidered chiffon (1978),
"Golden Thimble Award".

Opposite, a dress made of embroidered and feathered silk scarves. A pearl was stitched at the base of each hand-painted feather to attach it to the dress.

Pages 30–31, on the left, Tracy, one of our models, wearing a black and white dress that could be worn back to front as a tunic. It was the beginning of our passion for the Viennese painter Klimt. Right, Tracy again, in one of our first knitted, quilted coats, with an almost Balkan look. It is double-knitted in red, violet and blue, over a flowing dress in black and white printed crêpe de Chine, "Golden Thimble Award", 1978.

Pages 32–33, our American model Carol Alt, who inspired the house of Féraud for several years, wearing, on either side, two cotton dresses and, in the middle, a jersey skirt and jacket, 1979.

Pages 34–35, avant-garde in 1958; these colorful jersey dresses foreshadowed Courrèges, Mary Quant and the Swinging Sixties. The absence of zippers and the use of jersey symbolized women's search for greater freedom and heralded the liberated woman. Facing them on the right, a 1982 silk dress – the same spirit twenty years later, after a long voyage back to femininity.

went broke for the first time in my life. There was something almost exhilarating about it. I could already see myself painting seascapes on the quay in sunny Saint Tropez, selling a picture a day and playing "pétanque" (the game of bowls) under the plane trees. (Mia, a painter herself, had already bought me an easel and was beginning to think about what kind of palette to get me as well.)

Poverty lent me a sense of gravity and detachment that I had rarely experienced before: I felt there was probably a lesson to be learned from it. Upon reflection, I was reminded of my friend the Italian knitwear manufacturer. I had personally designed a line of sweaters – something between lace nightshirts and pullovers – for this man, and he paid me in marble statues carved by a cousin of his in Carrara. Although an American buyer bought the first 6,000 sweaters in a single morning, my Italian friend never sold another one after that. He was left broke, with a huge stock of unsold sweaters. Such are the vagaries of fashion . . . Later on, however, my friend finally hit the jackpot. He now lives in a thirty-room Florentine palazzo, sleeping in a different room every night. (His peculiar ideas of luxury somewhat disconcert his visiting lady friends and the maid, who complain that they feel as if they are rooming in a hotel!) He has switched to banking and now finances the sweater trade in and around Florence.

I realized that fashion, with its unpredictable swings, is like a game of chance, and that I had merely had an unlucky throw. Sure enough, my luck soon changed: In January 1984 our summer collection was awarded the Golden Thimble for the second time. This award, which at first had difficulty in getting off the ground, is now internationally coveted and – the ultimate accolade – imitated. It has even inspired the masters of the art of Chinese cuisine to create their own Golden Chopsticks award. Perhaps distinguished writers will soon be honored with a Golden Pen, and deserving plumbers will receive a Golden Wrench . . . Receiving the Golden Thimble was certainly a thrill. The day the award was announced, all work stopped at our "maison" on the Faubourg. Champagne corks were popping, and everyone was kissing everyone else. What a magnificent moment it was – one of those unexpected pleasures in the life of a "maison de couture."

A few days later Danièle Mitterand, France's first lady and our next-door neighbor, dropped in unexpectedly. She bought two suits – one black, the other navy – and borrowed a pair of my cufflinks. Monsieur le Président apparently had something up his sleeve. She told us that he was planning to honor French "couture" with an

Fashion is not created to separate people, but to bring them together –
it is a rendez-vous of love.

Pages 38–39, natural silk
dress, trimmed with lace
flounces. The square-brimmed
hat completes the geometric
lines of the design, 1982.

I could hardly have guessed then that I would be crossing

oceans more often than I do the Seine.

Page 36, a hand-knitted coat in black and white wool, evocative of the Queen of Diamonds.

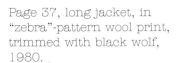

Page 37, long jacket, in "zebra"-pattern wool print, trimmed with black wolf, 1980.

Pages 40–41, dresses of the late seventies: embroidered natural silk, covered with printed velvet, satin and ribbons. The informality of the style which appeared at that time caused us to lose popularity with the media, which, no doubt, had grown accustomed to a more traditional "haute-couture" look.

Pages 42–43, the Spring/Summer Collection 1960 was shown in Acapulco at the Camino Real Hotel. Inspired by traditional Mexican fashion, the wedding gown of wool crêpe is covered with pastel-colored and black ribbons.

Dresses from our first public collection in 1952, photographed in 1980 for Louis Féraud's personal museum of "couture." Left, black lace dress with pleated chiffon. Right, pink silk jersey dress with matching pink rose and pearl-encrusted cuffs.

Pages 44–45, left, an evening dress embroidered on panne velvet and tulle. Right, a dress made of sequined fabric and tulle, embroidered with designs reminiscent of the French Art Deco painter Robert Delaunay, "Golden Thimble Award", 1984.

Left to right, Louis Féraud with two models, 1980 collection. Actress Mireille Darc in a 1965 petal dress of heavy silk crêpe. Above, Féraud with singer Mireille Mathieu; below, with Brigitte Bardot. With Sophie Derly, a model, wearing a boater and a smocked canvas coat, as photographed by Gilles Néret for the Japanese magazine "Chic."

official reception at the Elysée Palace. We were delighted: It was about time that our industry, which employs a quarter of a million people in France and brings in over a billion dollars in revenue each year from exports, got equal billing with the makers of champagne, Camembert and cars. The reception was a gala evening, and the "crème de la crème" had gathered in the great gilt Salon d' Honneur of the palace. When President Mitterand began his speech by announcing that he had some thoughts on "couture" that he wanted to share with us, we all held our breaths. Was he considering nationalizing the industry, or did he plan to issue a code of sartorial excellence for France's "fonctionnaires"? Neither. Instead, he began to discuss what he considered the artificial distinction often made between the "fine" and the "decorative" arts. In his opinion, fashion deserved its place in the pantheon of the fine arts alongside painting, sculpture, and architecture. He also might have added calligraphy, since our

invitations, bearing the gold-embossed Phrygian cap and Francisque – the emblems of the French Republic – were also handwritten in graceful italic script – a lovely gesture to the Magic Marker generation from a man who governs with a fountain pen.
The President ended his speech with an appropriately whimsical quote from the writer Louis Aragon, on the timelessness of fashion: "'Nana!' I exclaimed, 'your taste is in tune with the times.' 'No,' she protested, 'my taste is as timeless as the passing seasons. I give life to all that shines and shimmers, and what is doomed to oblivion falls in my wake. I am the Zeitgeist.'"

"Ladies and Gentlemen of fashion," Mitterand concluded with a toast, "you are the Zeitgeist of our times. May your creativity forever mark each passing season." It was a fitting homage to our fugitive profession, which tinkers with time and taste; this crazy profession that I still love as much as I love life and women.

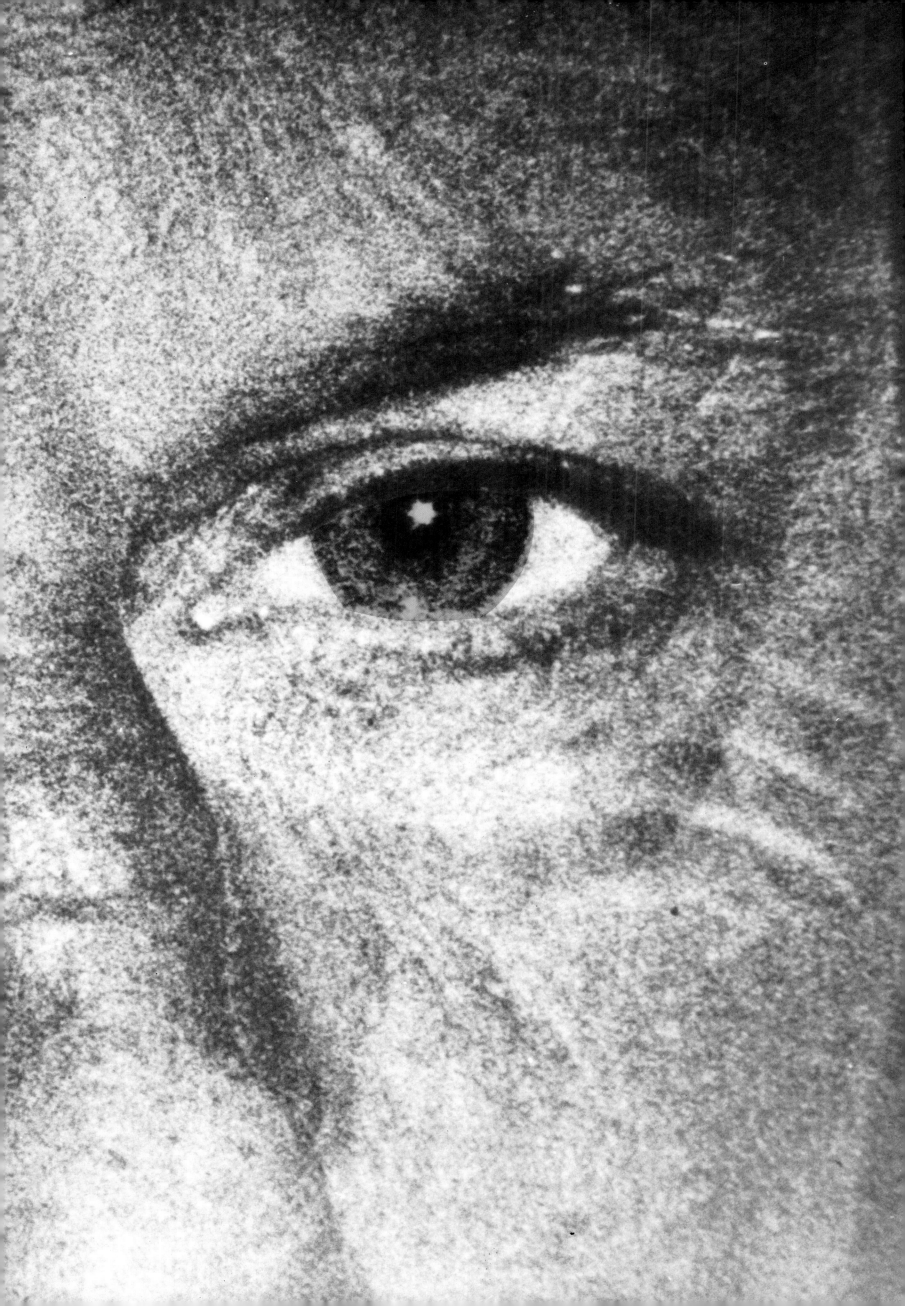

Sketches by Helga for the
Fall/Winter Collection
1983–84.

History of a Collection

Behind the elegant classical façade of the Maison Féraud on the Faubourg Saint Honoré in Paris, an army of a hundred people works feverishly year-round to design and produce two annual collections for presentation in January and July. A collection is no haphazard event. It takes months of careful planning and starts with a pile of drawings and a single proviso: No holds barred when it comes to creativity. Our stylists only have to be intensely creative twice a year – for the spring/summer and for the fall/winter collections – a demand that they meet with the furious commitment and élan of artists.

"Couture" is more than a profession, it is a vocation, and like all true vocations it has more to do with inspiration and talent than with education. While students can train their eyes and learn how to draw in art schools and fashion institutes, to become "couturiers" they would do just as well to stay at home and read Colette, Proust, or even Marx. We usually have a couple of people in our designers' studio who have been to art school – a shortcoming that they rapidly overcome in this most unacademic of professions.

I like to think of our "maison de couture" as a family. Zizi, my ever-present confidant, partner, and alter ego, has stayed by my side through thick and thin; and although she has trained the best of us – Esterel, Jean-Louis Scherrer, and Per Spook – she is still not really aware of her genius. When she starts dreaming out loud, however, we all pay close attention.

Caroline, our stylist from Wales, has one definite advantage over the rest of us: No one can understand her when she starts swearing in Welsh. Bernard, our would-be Don Juan, consoles himself at the end of each new romance by designing the menswear and some of the "haute couture." Helga, another of our creative forces, comes from Iceland; there is something almost evanescent about her, and her designs are imbued with a mysterious quality as well; perhaps the northern lights have inspired her fine sense of color. Besides her work on the collection, she is responsible for our designer sheets and towels as well as our swimwear, which is made in Italy.

While the rest of the staff is busy designing and preparing the collection, the "maison" is kept in order by Astrid, our young, dynamic German administrator. Alone, she handles the work of ten people and runs the export department, a difficult and at times thankless task without which the collection would never leave Paris. Meanwhile, we all work as a team in preparing the collection, selecting the music, and staging the entire production down to the

Pages 58–59, studies for patterns by Caroline, 1965.

Pages 60–61, "kite" dresses drawn by Helga. These designs were printed on satin, but were finally never used for dresses; instead, they were turned into interior design fabrics.

Integrity in fashion is

never pretending one knows,

because only time will tell.

Creating a new collection is like inventing a new language,

using a new alphabet, new words and an unfamiliar syntax.

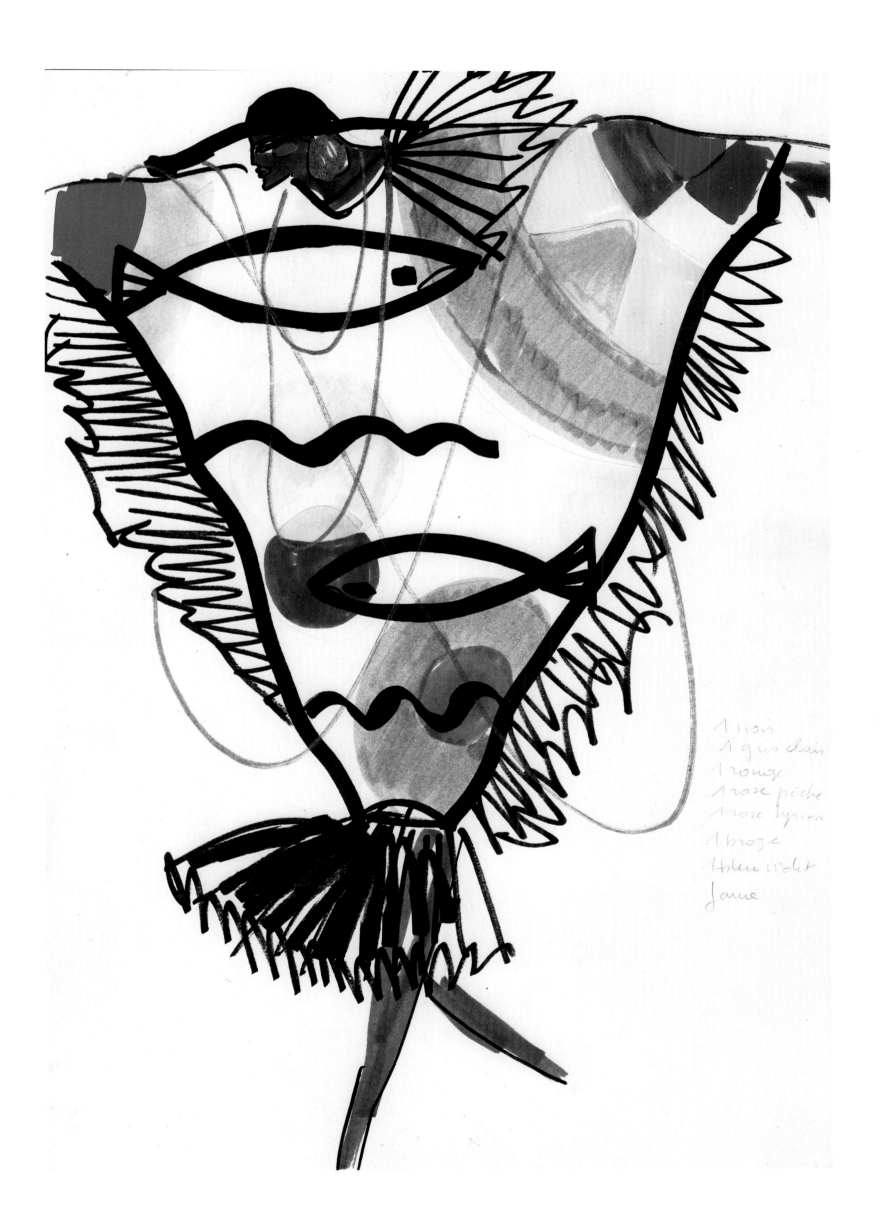

Caroline's variations on a
theme – the combination of
black and white graphics and
color.

the only thing we need to know is what does not yet exist

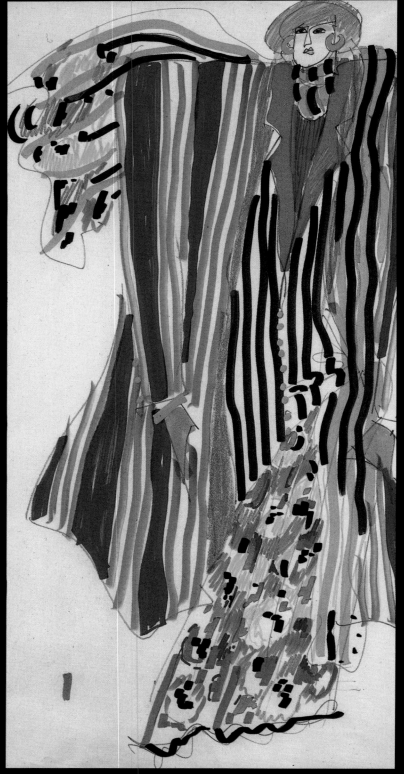
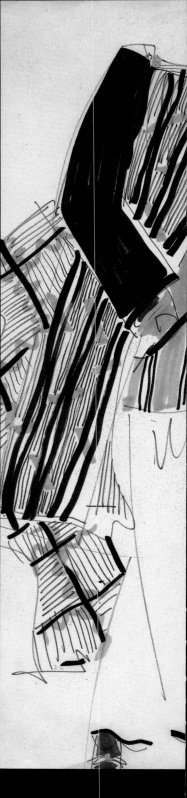

Chic is stronger and more fleeting than elegance

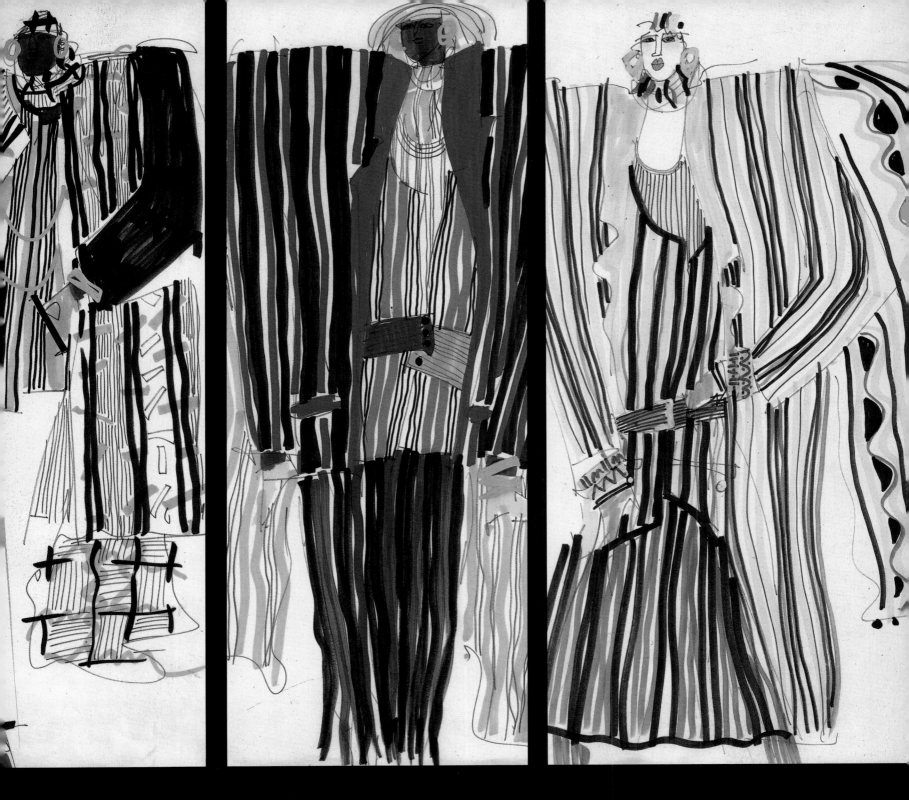

It doesn't reassure. It is sharp and precise, like the blade of a knife.

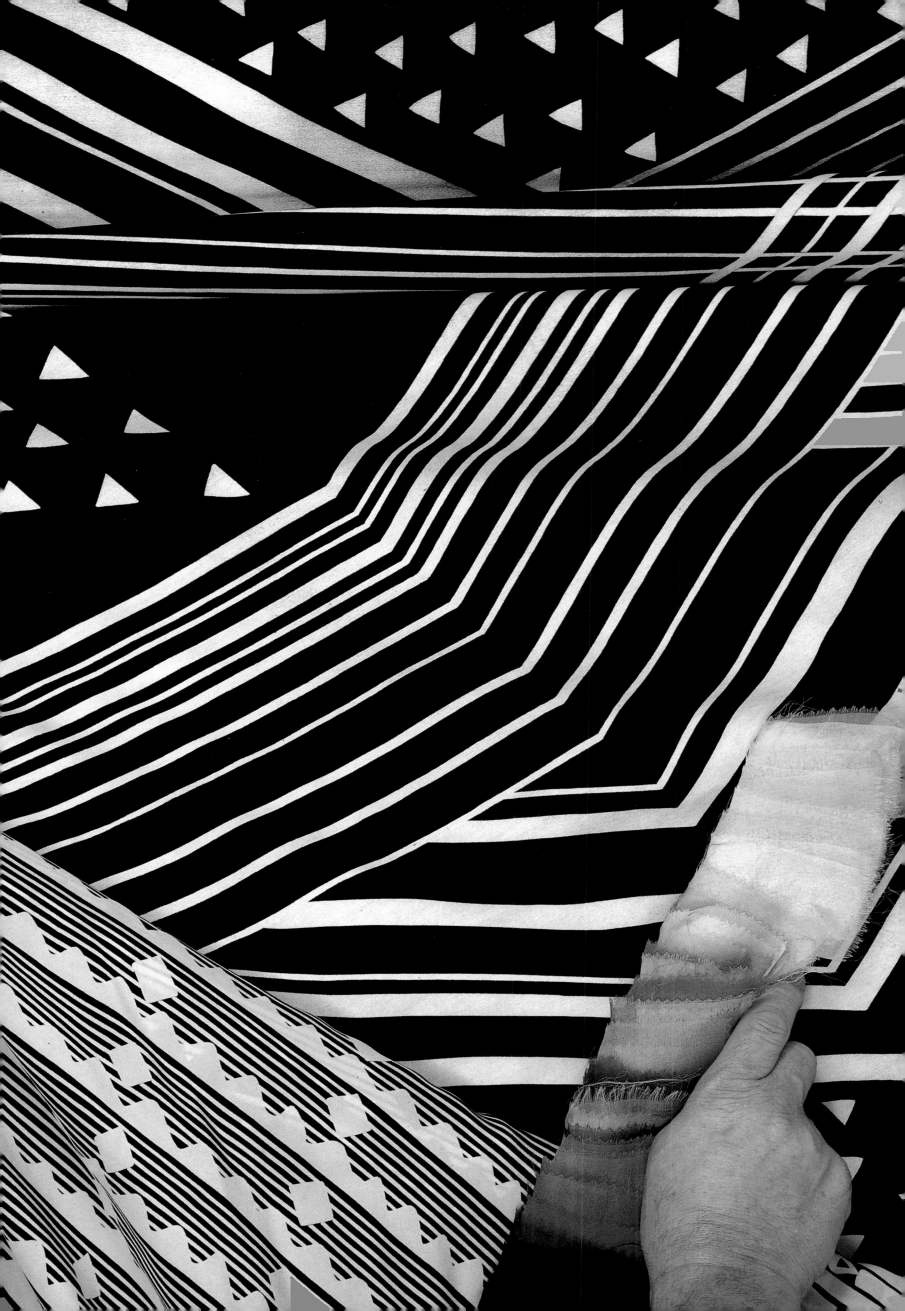

Drawing is to fashion what a blueprint is to architecture – a dress, like an eighteenth-century palace, often looks better on paper than when it is completed. However, in 1970, we managed to successfully translate the red butterflies on Bernard's hats into "prêt à porter."

Pages 64–65, a mixture of printed fabrics. Each pattern is printed on at least three different backgrounds. Five ranges of colors are applied to each of these backgrounds, while the initial pattern is done in at least fifteen different projections. Sometimes we even print over already printed fabrics, one pattern superimposed on another. The outfit sketched is a suit, blouse and skirt, 1982.

Pages 66–69, sketches by Caroline for the Spring/Summer Collection 1985. The printing techniques developed for 1985 are a complete departure from fabric design as it has been practised since 1945. The fruit, flowers and stripes drawn by Caroline are all set against a white background. The technique used is similar to that of porcelain painting. The contrast between the color and the white is striking.

Pages 70–71: When the bolts of printed fabric finally arrive, they must be matched, and color added. Wasp-waisted culotte-dress worn under a skirt made of "fermière" satin – a type of satin used in French peasant dresses – printed on shantung, 1981.

Pages 72–73, dresses from the Spring/Summer Collection 1981, in geometric-patterned satin crêpe.

82.

The most successful pieces owe their radiance to desire.

Above, preliminary sketches by Helga for the Fall/Winter Collection 1983.

Pages 76–77: In 1966 we finally succumbed to the mini-skirt. But we tried to avoid the inflexibility of the trend, adapting it to our flowing, comfortable style. Left, an evening gown, entirely covered with navy, white and pink sequins. Right, wool crêpe dresses in black and white.

Pages 78–79, silk dresses in geometric patterns, 1981. In fashion, geometry should blend sensuality with elegance of form.

last detail. Once the designs leave the drawing boards of our young and, at times, temperamental stylists, they undergo constant transformations and modifications, right up to the day when our models finally parade the outfits down the runway under blazing spotlights. Each highly skilled craftsman involved in the actual production of the collection is backed up by at least two no less talented professionals working to keep the line and the house moving. The staff includes administrators, accountants, salespeople, packers, dressers, models, photographers, graphic artists, and last but not least, the messenger boys.

As the day of the collection draws nearer and tempers grow shorter, the messengers become more and more important to us. They rush back and forth between the design studios and the workrooms, crisscrossing Paris several times a day in all kinds of weather. They are our Pony Express. Without the messengers, work would come to a standstill, since they are our lifeline to the subcontractors – embroiderers, jewelers, furriers, and shoemakers – whose services are critical to the collection. They also replenish the endless supply of cigarettes and coffee we need to keep going. The messengers bear the goods and the good tidings. A completed outfit is a victory over the clock, and each glittering gown owes its existence

as much to their speed and diligence as to the combined craft and
creativity of the rest of the staff.

   Like the other Paris fashion houses, Féraud is part of the "haute
couture" industry – a prestigious and highly idiosyncratic field. And
to ensure that it stays that way, the Chambre Syndicale (the
"couturiers" association, which is reminiscent of a medieval guild)
maintains strict control over the profession. The sense of
anachronism runs deep: in fact, the Chambre has been compared to
an Italian republic straight out of the Renaissance. Though there is
not as much intrigue in the Chambre as there was in the Medicis'
Italy, there is definitely something conspiratorial about the way the
members of the Chambre operate behind a veil of secrecy to avoid
divulging any of our trade secrets. Also like the Italian republics, we
rely on a mixture of chance, stealth, and calculated risk in order to
survive. In fact, successfully running a fashion house and preparing a
collection depends as much on chance as on creative flair.

   Creating a new collection is like inventing a new language using a
new alphabet, new words, and an unfamiliar syntax. At a certain
point, one begins to feel tongue-tied and helpless. Memory and past
knowledge become cumbersome: In our profession, the only thing we
need to know is what does not yet exist.

Pages 80–81, left, sheer dress
in raw silk. Right, leopard and
flower print on chiffon. Carol
was a true professional. She
would take hours to prepare
for each shooting, carefully
applying her makeup and
following the hairdresser's
every move. The mixture of
print and transparence makes
her look strong and fragile at
the same time.

Pages 82–83, sketches by
Caroline, 1979.

Pages 84–89, sketches by
Bernard.

Pages 90–91, two patterns on crêpe de Chine (1977–78) vividly contrasting an abstract flower on the left with the natural one on the right. The background geometric designs are hand-drawn.

Pages 92–93, patterned suits and coats made from Tibetan fabrics, 1984. The inside of the coat and dress are copies of an original pattern on crêpe de Chine printed in Lyons. Journalists noted a Precolumbian influence in these designs. At least they were right about the altitude. The mountain peoples of the Himalayas and the Andes produce strikingly similar designs.

Each new collection must be completely different from the previous one and yet at the same time no one should be aware of this. I have to make certain that this apparent contradiction goes unnoticed. Like Narcissus, I must be reflected in every detail of the collection – without, however, becoming submerged in self-indulgence. I do not underestimate the risks involved. Starting a new collection is like driving up to a busy intersection that has no traffic lights, or more simply, like jumping off a cliff.

Recently, for example, I was walking through the salon where we prepare the collection, when I had a shock. Our head stylist Caroline was fitting a model with a strange new garment – always a good sign, since the most revolutionary changes in fashion generally begin with something that looks totally outlandish at first. I realized that the woman trying on the outfit was none other than Astrid, who has been with us for fifteen years. I hadn't even recognized her. The dress, shaped like an elongated potato sack, had a train at least four yards long and was completely encrusted with "diamonds." As a finishing touch Astrid had been fitted with a blond wig and a mink-covered felt hat. The overall effect was stunning. Caroline, no doubt anticipating my objections on grounds of marketability, told me that this vision, which she had come up with over lunch, was the image of the new woman – bold and romantic.

The dress was indeed tremendously new and elegant. But would it please our clients? No amount of marketing studies could answer that question. Reflecting on this, I took out my Polaroid to see if I could capture on film the novelty of the silhouette before me. The next day I

Ready for the shot. Right,
photographer Hervé Nabon
working with Carol Alt in his
studio.

Pages 96–97, backstage at the
fashion house where confusion
reigns at collection time. On
the wall, at the right, designs
that have already gone to the
workrooms. While we're
pulling our hair out, the
overworked seamstresses keep
remarkably calm.

would look at the picture and decide. In the meantime Astrid, who
had been standing in front of the mirror for half an hour, was gazing
dreamily at her reflection, which seemed to have taken on a life of its
own. Although in fact she was probably only thinking about her little
boy, waiting impatiently at home for his mother to return from work,
I knew then that I would include the dress in the collection.

Charles Frédéric Worth was the first to come up with the idea of
creating a collection of women's fashions each season and using live
models to present it to the public. That was back in 1858. Since then,
things have not stopped changing. Over the past twenty-five years
I've seen English flannel manufactured in Italy (with all due respect)
and blue foxes raised in cages like chickens. But more than a century
after Worth's first collection, "couturiers" still work in much the same
way he did in his time, or even as the "couturiers" did in the days of
Louis XIV. Even with the computer, the art of drawing has not
demonstrably changed since Raphael. What are constantly changing
today are the collections' sources of inspiration.

For one of our latest collections, for example, we sent our top
stylists, Caroline and Helga, to Tibet to look for new forms, colors, and
ideas. The trip was a success, and the resulting collection – fall/winter
1984/85 – an enormous hit. However, the collection was "officially"
inspired by Sicily! Such are the inscrutable ways of the muses of
fashion. Why Sicily? For some inexplicable reason, we had decided
that it was time to return to the spirit of romanticism. Perhaps we
had felt a collective yearning for drama; something brash and bold to
transcend incipient libertinage (and those ubiquitous grays and

however, becoming submerged in self-indulgence.

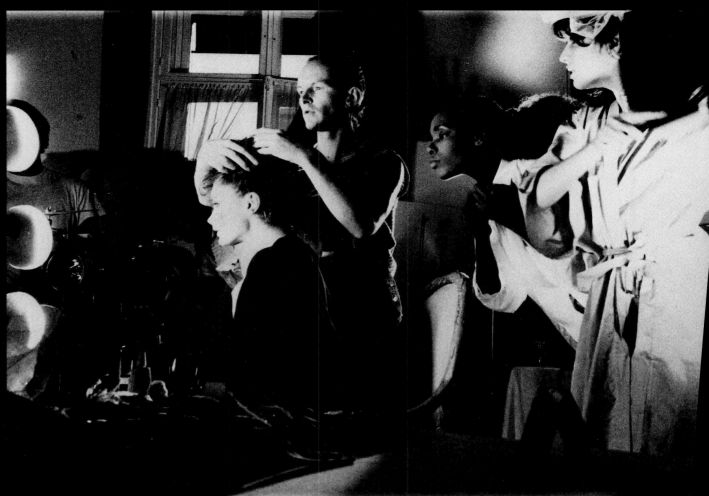

Ideas are the only commodity.

a tiresome feeling of indifference.

Getting ready for the collection,
everything from hanging curtains to
setting up the runway. Checking for
last-minute details, making up the
models, testing the lights and music. In
terms of theater, the Comédie Française
has nothing on the presentation of a
collection, for fashion relies on many of
the same devices. Here, we were
filming for American television. The
room looks like a Habsburg palace – in
fact, it was in Paris. The
eighteenth-century interior dome had
windows with a splendid view of Paris,
which had been blocked out. The
director decided to use a diagonal laser
beam as a curtain. The models were
supposed to cross this curtain of light,
shouting. I was out front, surrounded
by billowing smoke which turned green
and blue in the light from the laser
beam. It took days of hard work to
make this film, which ended up as a
30-second spot. Each shot was
endlessly cut and recut. The entire
production took place in total darkness,
pierced by flashes of dazzling light. It
was in this atmosphere of blinding light
and deafening sound that I had my first
encounter with American film-making
on the other side of the screen – its
precision, speed and efficiency.

garment and a woman's body.

blacks), and to overcome a tiresome feeling of indifference. The figure that had most inspired our interest was the aristocratic Sicilian count, hero of Tomasi di Lampedusa's popular novel "The Leopard," who had been magnificently portrayed on the screen by Burt Lancaster. We designed a collection for his kind of woman – strong, willful, and feminine – a passionate woman who would not take infidelity lightly.

Whether a collection is inspired by Brazil, Tibet, or Sicily, it must always obey the same inescapable laws. From conception to presentation, it must progress like clockwork according to a precise schedule. The process begins with a brainstorming session with the stylists and thirty sketches. We also decide on a palette of about ten colors. Copies of each design are developed in five different colors, and each color is tested on a variety of fabrics – satin, muslin, cotton, and wool. Sometimes we choose printed fabrics, such as Japanese silks striped in matching tones, on which to print the chosen patterns in different colors. Then again, we might try using more structured fabrics, such as velvets that have undergone "discharge" printing (in which some of the original hues are replaced by acid colors) or "etching" (in which part of the fabric's pile is burned away using chemicals, leaving near-transparent patterned areas). We try even more elaborate techniques such as pigmentation, which leaves a solid residue of color on the surface of the fabric, giving it a boardlike finish. This first phase is very important, since everything depends on the quality and originality of the patterns and prints.

Over the years our fashion house has become a veritable factory for fabric design. You don't have to go to art school to realize that ever since Monet and the Impressionists, light has been tantamount to form. And fabric design, like painting, is a matter of learning how to play with light and shadow. I like to pattern velvet so that the silk or cotton weave shows through the fabric, giving our dresses a feeling of lightness and transparency that has become our trademark. Velvet works beautifully when it is used to ornament and highlight the line and movement of a dress.

The artist Duroux (winner of the Prix de Rome for sculpture) translates our drawings into prints, using techniques identical to those employed in printing a lithograph or an art book. He supervises the preparation of the colors that are applied to the fabrics by plate or roller. He carefully measures out the thickening agents, mostly organic, to prevent the dyes from running and to maintain the crispness of the original prints.

Matching coat and dress, 1982. The prints, by Caroline and Helga, are combined with dyed blue fox. The base fabric was silk, threaded with gold and silver. During the printing process the silk threads took on the reflections of the gold thread.

There is something exciting and at the same time daunting about the almost infinite variety of fabric designs that can be produced by combining pattern and color. No less frightening is the feeling we have – like a painter in front of his blank canvas – when the first 400 bolts of printed fabric come back from the factory. Faced with such a mountain of cloth, I always feel like running away to a desert island. But that is only the beginning, since it will all have to be combined with nearly as many yards of plain fabric, knits, and leathers before the collection is completed. At this point, eleven weeks remain before the presentation, and I can still allow myself a nervous breakdown, provided it doesn't last longer than half a day.

Now the theme of the collection is no longer as obvious as when we began. We start to panic as the entire selection process begins all over again: This time we have to produce the actual working drawings – 500 of them – from which a single design will be retained. From this sketch another batch of 500 drawings is prepared. Now only 250 new drawings are required to produce the final three designs upon which the entire collection will be based.

From this point on, the intuitive process gives way to deductive reasoning as the designs are sent to the heads of the workrooms so that they can produce the "toiles," or prototypes, of the garments in rough cotton. These "toiles" are then tried on two ravishing models who have been especially chosen to serve as guinea pigs during the long and painstaking fittings required to prepare each garment. The "toiles" are the quintessential tool of the "couturier." Looking at them, he must be able to imagine their metamorphosis into the final garment, whose folds, drape, line, and movement must be precisely gauged before it is actually made. The original sketches are now but a vague memory in the progress from concept to reality. The most crucial moment in the preparation of the collection has arrived: The garment emerges to face praise or disapproval. It must stand on its own.

Next comes what I call the ballet of accessories. A new breed of hat suddenly appears in the millinery workrooms. A cache of unusual belts is discovered in a Parisian attic where a devotee of doeskin has been working in obscurity for thirty years. The ordered jewels arrive; unfortunately, they don't work, and others have to be designed. The jewelry designer threatens to commit suicide, but with the help of a few "kirs" and some cajoling, she gives up the idea and agrees to redo the jewelry. Only twenty-nine days left. Ashtrays fill up and bottles empty. You'd think you were in Montparnasse in the days of Modigliani.

Knitted dresses, "Golden Thimble Award", 1984.

Pages 110–111, two evening gowns in printed silk; left, embroidered and pearled. Right, silk gauze, gilded with fine golden thread, 1982.

Extravagance is when the medium takes over. Elegance is when

the message remains polite.

116

Three embroidered, pearled, silk gowns, "Golden Thimble Award", 1984.

Pages 112–113, left, an evening gown of panne velvet lamé, "Golden Thimble Award" 1983. Right, four printed, embroidered and pearled dresses. Dresses should be extravagant. In a tailored suit a woman's figure is flattered less than in a voluptuous drapery. In fashion, the sensual should always take precedence, and drapery, like a flowing river, is the most sensual form a dress can be given. Leonardo da Vinci compared the currents in a river to a woman's hair.

Pages 114–115, lace dresses, 1979. Lace, like the "fascinator" veil on the left, adds to the mystery and delicacy of a woman.

Like a writer uses punctuation, a designer uses accessories as an indispensable device for setting off detail and providing accent and clarity to his creations. Buttons, belts, buckles, fringes, tassles, epaulettes, not to mention handbags, scarves, hats, and shoes, must harmonize with each outfit's basic components: jacket, top, skirt, or dress. From the model's stockings to her eyelashes, the entire ensemble must be coherent and in character. When it is time to "accessorize" an outfit, we are faced with dozens of bewildering possibilities from which we must select combinations of accessories to accent and vary the main themes. Even computer circuits would blow up under such a strain – but a "couturier" must keep his cool.

I keep calm by contemplating the dream girls as they try on the pieces in the collection. They all must be at least five-feet-eight-inches tall, ideally five-eleven. Anyone shorter is unceremoniously sacked. A model's most important feature is the length of her back. She should measure an unusually long foot and a half from the small of her back to her last cervical vertebra. Models are chosen more for their stylized or sophisticated looks than for beauty or poise. An exaggerated silhouette, not unlike the almost surreal figure immortalized by Ingres in his "Grande Odalisque," is deliberately sought. When that painting was first unveiled, the critics reproached Ingres for his "mannerism" and for adding three extra vertebrae to the model's neck, but for a designer, a woman's neck is never too long. Like Ingres, he must be willing to break the canons of "realism" and stretch line and proportion to achieve a desired effect. A designer's craft is evident in the most subtle details – the way a necklace follows the curve of a neck, the sensuous encounter of breast and bodice, or the delicate lines of long, gloved arms. The most successful pieces in a collection often owe their radiance to the inspiration of desire.

Preparing the collection keeps our three workrooms running at full steam. While the "flouteuses" (the women in charge of sewing soft, loose garments) turn out the dresses, the "tailleuses," who work on the more structured garments, painstakingly "construct" suits and coats. Some suits are easy to make, while others (which may have taken up to three months of work to produce) sometimes end up being scrapped. During this intense phase of continual fittings, we keep the air conditioning turned up so the models won't faint; between fittings they put on furs, even in midsummer, to avoid catching cold.

The messengers rush in from the airport with three parcels from Italy. These contain "English" flannel, two yards of printed leather

Left, satin gown in embroidered and pearled satin, "Golden Thimble Award" 1984.

dyed in Caroline and Helga's "Tibetan" colors, and sixty pairs of shoes. We open the parcels and continue combining accessories. Other leathers emerge from the storeroom, printed with the same pattern as the bolts of chiffon destined to be made into blouses and scarves – the necessary coordinates for the so-called passages, or groups of outfits displayed on the runway. In watching films of previous collections, I realized that the public enjoys seeing ten or twelve models advancing in formation along the runway, creating the effect of a leisurely promenade or a street scene.

We always work to music, and when the music pouring out of the loudspeakers catches someone's fancy, we immediately dispatch a messenger to the radio station to find out the name of the song. Within minutes he returns with the answer: It is the theme song from "The Godfather." Unanimously, we decide to use it as background music for the presentation, and in order to stay in the spirit we all don Borsalino hats someone has unearthed from one of the storerooms. Disguised as mafiosi, we continue our frenetic battle with time.

The large "couture" workrooms with two to three hundred people disappeared after Poiret and Dior. Nowadays, we all subcontract a good part of the work. The furs are made by furriers who in turn are permitted to distribute or retail our label. Embroidery is also done in specialized houses. Since it takes at least four weeks to embroider an evening gown, and there is only a month before the presentation, we must decide how we are going to do the finale of the collection. Should we embroider and "feather" our prints on the gowns, or should we choose from among over 250 samples of embroidery that have been submitted by five of the foremost specialized houses? This time, we decide to have our own designs embroidered in white on white chiffon by the firm Broderies de Provence, famous for its lacework, in the medieval town of Manosque. Since time is running out, the fittings take place at the provincial airport of Miramas, near Manosque, no doubt the first time the finale of a fashion show has ever been put together in an airport lounge.

During the last four days of the countdown, everything suddenly becomes very still, as if we were in the eye of a storm. As the outfits emerge one by one from the workrooms to be tried on for the tenth time, we add the accessories and jewelry and begin our first dress rehearsal. The presentation is rehearsed in miniature in our salon on a fifteen-yard runway, less than half the length of the one used on the

Right, a wedding gown from the first large collection presented to the public in 1958. White, the color of innocence, accompanies a woman through every phase of her life, from her First Communion to her baby's crib.

Embroidered dresses at the finale of the 1984 "Golden Thimble Award" ceremony. These are "computer" dresses, covered with tiny, transparent glass chips that are stitched with multi-colored thread. The transparency softens the color, making it almost pastel. The dresses are trimmed with three hundred mirror shards.

Pages 122–123, finale of the 1982 collection. A wedding gown of embroidered and pearled georgette crêpe. The bridesmaids are wearing printed silk.

day of the collection. As we sit watching in anguish, the models parade each outfit in front of us. For the first time we see the overall look of the collection and are surprised and relieved. It looks wonderful, with the exception of a few outfits that seem to have been created in a moment of madness. We step back as far as possible to get a better perspective. It still looks good, even though it's two in the morning and the room is full of cigarette smoke.

In the night before the collection, the house is in pandemonium. All of the outfits seem to pour out of the workrooms at once. The dressers run in circles around our eighteen models, who are busy trying to find a tube of lipstick or a lost eyelash. Endlessly, the tape of the music starts, stops, and is run back in order to synchronize the passages during this final rehearsal. Caroline kneels beside the seamstresses to help sew colored roses onto the wedding gown according to the original sketch. In these few remaining hours during the middle of the night, we rush to make last-minute changes and to add the finishing touches to the collection.

The first set of outfits to appear on the runway is crucial. They must be an absolute knockout. The public should immediately discern the style of the new woman we have created for the season. Once the first group of outfits has been shown, we know from experience that luck and improvisation take over and the entire presentation acquires a rhythm of its own. The medium becomes the message. One hundred and ten outfits, totaling over 350 pieces with the assorted ensembles – hats, bags, jewels, and shoes – will be presented in a matter of fifty minutes to an audience of over 1,000 people.

Backstage, five hairdressers, half-a-dozen makeup artists, fifteen dressers, and three "accessorists" prepare the first group of models to step out onto the runway and into the spotlight for the collection's first passage. I give the lighting technician his cue, and the house is plunged into darkness. The music soars, and the spotlights form two bright circles, which merge to create a heart. And the magic ritual begins once again.

From Haute Couture
to Industry

My work as a designer begins

with a woman in search of comfort and freedom.

The world of accessories: stockings and shoes by Louis Féraud. A shoe is a very telling object. Many old ideas have found refuge in shoes: although the monarchy fell, the Louis XV heel survived. Each time elegance and sophistication disappear, the heel goes with them. Personally, I love women in bare feet. But if a woman wants to put on heels, she should wear them to bed. I am not against a woman wearing her Louis XV heels to go to sleep.

Pages 126–127, 130–133, Louis Féraud ready-to-wear factories in Germany (Darmstadt) and Italy (Turin).

Pages 136–137, furs. Left natural fox; right, dyed fox. Dyed fox is the ghost of a fox.

In our society, what does not grow and change is doomed to extinction. In this constantly changing and competitive world, once the house of Louis Féraud had made the quantum leap from a cottage industry to a "maison de couture," I realized that if we wanted not only to survive but to thrive, I had to expand our fashion house.

In order to expand a fashion house effectively these days, you have to create a multinational corporation. For us this meant making Paris the headquarters of a network of affiliates and subsidiaries based in nearly every industrialized country. Each of our subsidiaries is bound by contract to maintain the high standards of our line, to promote it in the style we decree, and to conform to our unified advertizing strategy.

Like most other labor-intensive industries over the past twenty years, the clothing industry – one of the world's largest – has migrated toward the Far East. Clothes can be manufactured in Singapore, Hong Kong, and South Korea for considerably less than in Europe or North America. Along with the unprecedented growth of the textile industry and its migration to newly emerging economies, the world of fashion has seen yet another and perhaps more remarkable mutation stemming from economic and social changes in Western societies.

Nowadays clothes are looked upon as "expendable" and, next to food, as the least durable of goods. By comparison, a car is made to last at least five years, while a piece of clothing remains an eminently perishable commodity. One might wear an out-of-fashion dress, but few people would buy one, with the possible exception of nostalgia freaks or habitués of the Salvation Army. One reason for this significant change in attitude has been the emergence of large numbers of affluent young consumers who represent a dominant force in the marketplace. Their ever-increasing demand for innovative products and their unpredictable buying patterns pose enormous challenges to anyone who aspires to success in the design, production, marketing, and promotion of clothing.

In 1960, we launched our first "prêt à porter" collection with three major outlets in France. We signed twenty more licenses with Japan, while at Saks we were destined to remain the "leaders" from 1958 to 1970 – with all the shop-window space and publicity that that implied. Louis Féraud ready-to-wear fashions are now available in 300 stores throughout the United States and Canada – in thirty-seven branches of Saks Fifth Avenue, Neiman-Marcus, I. Magnin, Bonwit Teller, Bergdorf Goodman, Holt Renfrew, and Sakowitz – from the Atlantic to the Pacific.

Louis
adore le
Du haut ju
Du bas jusq
Collants L

Les collants Louis Féra

Fame is a collection of good manners without which a label cannot become a name.

éraud
emmes.
u'aux bas.
ux collants.
is Féraud.

t en Ergelan® anti-plis.

The "Louis Féraud Adores Women" advertizing campaign, created by Jean Feldman and photographed by Just Jaekin, 1970.

A study of coordination between cars and clothes, 1970.

Louis Féraud sunglasses, 1972.

"Storyboard" ads: Louis Féraud boots on a motorcycle and the first perfumes, "Justine" and "Corrida", 1970.

The Japanese distribute
windsurf boards all over the
Far East. We design the sails.
For us, a windsurfer should
feel like he is on a luxury liner.

Which came first? The sail or
the dress. Drawings by
Bernard.

computer, the art of drawing has not demonstrably changed since Raphael.

painter, a designer must be willing to break the canons of "realism"

a desired effect.

Perfume,

a woman's

invisible signature.

Between 1965 and 1975, we signed licensing agreements for over forty products with ninety-seven different companies throughout the world. These ninety-seven licenses were the beginning of an extraordinary adventure that continues today – a marriage of French creativity with German, American, and Japanese efficiency that has made Féraud number one in women's ready-to-wear inspired by "haute couture."

Today each presentation of our "prêt à porter," inspired by the "haute couture" collection, is an international event that attracts the media and buyers from all over the world. We owe this success not only to our desire to provide people with clothes that are elegant and easy to wear, but also to our ability to adapt to the tastes and cultures of the countries with which we work. For example, our relationship with Japan has evolved over the years in its own inimitable manner. Our first "operation" began twenty-five years ago when my Japanese partners "locked me up" in a hotel belonging to the Seibu department store group so that I could design, on the spot, a collection for the modern Japanese woman. I chose Kazuko Matsuda, one of the most famous Japanese models, as the star of my collection, and the Seibu group put hundreds of workers at my disposal, along with 3,000 yards of fabric that I hastily selected.

In the streets of Kyoto, hired storytellers clambered onto discarded packing crates and told old Japanese legends to attentive groups of young and old people. Every now and then they would weave "plugs" for the Seibu department stores and for my collection into their stories. Fate ran its course, and the collection was a great success. The following week, dozens of manufacturers came to me. Japan had adopted me and the Féraud line.

Our second Japanese period was born of that American innovation, the science of marketing. Since the dawn of the Meiji Revolution over a century ago, the Japanese, caught between East and West, have been trying to decode the language of Western fashion, exploring what defines Western chic, elegance, glamour, look, line. Nevertheless, when they return from work in the evening, the Japanese exchange their business suits, uniforms, and overalls for printed cotton kimonos. To most Westerners the Japanese seem full of contradictions; to us they were the ideal testing market for our new lines in children's clothes, household linens, and glasses. In exchange, we readily provided them with fashions that they avidly transformed and adapted to their own tastes and culture.

My first trip to Japan and my first meeting with the Seibu group in 1958. Photograph by Gilles Néret.

Pages 140–141, Bernard's sketches for the 1984 menswear collection, made and distributed by the Gruppo Finanziario Tessile of Turin. A man's suit should be light, warm and comfortable or light, cool and comfortable. In the film "American Gigolo" Richard Gere flings his suits all over the bed, in what was no doubt an inspired insight by the director into men's attitudes towards fashion.

Pages 142–143, a collection of Louis Féraud sweaters. A study of stitches and colors by Bernard for the Fall/Winter 1985 collection of mohair sweaters made in Italy.

Pages 148–149, sketches for bathroom tiles coordinated with linen. Drawings by Bernard. The swimwear collection, designed by Helga.

Pages 150–151, an ad for the perfume "Fantasque". The Louis Féraud watch and costume jewelry were made by Avon in the U.S.A. in 1983.

We still have a lot to learn from Japan. For example, my associates there recently opened an avant-garde store. It is very large, well-located, and spacious, but there is nothing for sale – no machines, no consumer products. Ideas are the store's only commodity. This, they maintain, is the first step into the next century, when technology will have outpaced consumption. Perhaps someday they will sell lifestyles. In any case, our experience in Japan has enabled us to deal more serenely with markets in the rest of the world.

Nowadays, for instance, I often find myself in the uncomfortable position of having to remind others "I told you so," as I witness the worldwide swing back to classical values in fashion. For the past twenty-five years I have stayed the course, despite critics who have derided my "figurative" collections, my obstinate defense of a "feminine" look, and my attachment to traditional sources of inspiration, which goes back, no doubt, to my origins in that colorful but conservative corner of France, Arles.

Alternately, journalists will sometimes ask me, with great earnestness, what next year's look for women will be. For them I am supposed to be some kind of medium, capable of communicating with spirits and seeing into the future. After working in this industry for the past twenty-five years, I have arrived at a more modest view of my role: Like Marshall MacLuhan, I believe that the "medium is the message"; and that my task in the Louis Féraud company is to ensure that, instead of statements, what we make are beautiful clothes – clothes that make women beautiful. If I communicate with spirits, it is only with those of my friends and our stylists, and it is invariably to urge them never to forget their "joie de vivre."

Red Square, Moscow. Tamara, star ballerina of the Bolshoi, models a Louis Féraud outfit in front of the Church of Saint Basil, 1968. Photograph by Guy Rambaldi.

These lampion dresses make
the future seem as if it had
already happened. Black satin
bubble over short black velvet
sheath with dramatic glittery
belt. Fall/Winter Collection
1985–86.

Le Fér

88 Rue d   ubourg   ain